the **LOGIC** *of* **OPPOSITES**

Books by Alane Rollings

Transparent Landscapes (1984)

In Your Own Sweet Time (1989)

The Struggle to Adore (1994)

the LOGIC of OPPOSITES

ALANE ROLLINGS

TRIQUARTERLY BOOKS
NORTHWESTERN UNIVERSITY PRESS

Evanston, Illinois

TriQuarterly Books
Northwestern University Press
Evanston, Illinois 60208-4210

Copyright © 1998 by Alane Rollings. Published 1998 by TriQuarterly Books/Northwestern University Press. All rights reserved.

Printed in the United States of America

ISBN 0-8101-5081-6 (cloth)
ISBN 0-8101-5082-4 (paper)

Rollings, Alane, 1950–
      The logic of opposites / Alane Rollings.
      p. cm.
      ISBN 0-8101-5081-6 (alk. paper). — ISBN 0-8101-5082-4 (pbk. : alk. paper)
      I. Title.
   PS3568.0539L64 1998
   811'.54—dc21   98-5806
                                                                                                          CIP

For Dr. Edward A. Wolpert
for the rain control

For Dick
forever after

Contents

Part II

Acknowledgments

I would like to thank the editors of the following journals and anthologies in which some of these poems first appeared:

The Chicago Review, "The Outback"
Denver Quarterly, "Chopsticks on a Vase"
The Gettysburg Review, "The Uncontrollability of Things"; "To Be a Different Person"
Graven Images, "Forever After"
The North Atlantic Review, "Heaven's Extravagance"
North Dakota Quarterly, "Down the Interstate"; "The Day All Sides Claim Victory"
Outsiders, an anthology from Milkweed Press, "For Dear Life"
Poetry Calendar, "Unsafe Havens"
Prairie Schooner, "Pick Up the Pieces"; "Savannah"
Tamaqua, "Spiraling Upward"; "Unsafe Havens"; "Designing Heaven"
Third Coast, "Action at a Distance"; "Asking for More"; "Savages Taught Me"; "We Could Swim in It"
TriQuarterly, "The Logic of Opposites"; "The Substance of Evanescent Things"; "In Touching Distance"; "Gold Rush: 1848/1996"; "Positions of Strength"

My deep and constant gratitude to my husband, Richard Stern, whose brilliant magnanimity has been the sine qua non for all my books.

Heartfelt thanks to my other terrific readers, especially my invaluable friend Jody Stewart, and friends Leslie Miller, Patricia Goedicke, and Leilani Wright. Also to Nancy Eimers, Rosellen Brown, Lola Haskins, Lee McCarthy, Molly Bendall, Laure-Anne Bosselaar, Martha Friedberg, and *many* other marvelous women poets for their generosity and examples. I have large debts to Eleanor Lerman and Lynda Hull for their indelible inspiration and beauty.

Thanks to David Brooks in *Sheep and the Diva* for an idea for "Unsafe Havens." Also to Walter Becker in "Eleven Tracks of Whack" for a line and inspiration for "Hell and Up," and Josephine Humphreys in *Rich in Love* and Sting in "Ten Summoners' Tales" for two lines for "While Morning's Part of Night."

Thanks for special kindnesses to Richard Strier, Molly McQuade, Katy Carlitz, Bin Ramke, Ted and Virginia Solotaroff, Mark Perlberg, Bill Olsen, David Wojahn, Peter Wild, Peter Stitt, and Reginald Gibbons. To Regan Heiserman, an artist whose work and friendship have improved this book significantly, special thanks.

And to my wonderful, steadfast parents, Harry Evan Rollings and Irma Lee Pittman Rollings, my never-ending love and gratitude.

Part I

For mine's beyond beyond.
— Shakespeare, *Cymbeline*

Down the Interstate

*His left hand is under my head
and his right hand doth embrace me.*

— Song of Solomon 2:6

We needed guarantees we couldn't have
on the happiness we would.
　　You said we'd build a house in some village near a town
like the ones I'd summered in when I was young:
Ponchatoula; Petal; Thunderbolt.
　　Any of those enclaves in the landscape
where people fish hip-deep,
casting lines into the shimmer of ebb tide;
any of my onetime haunts still flickering on the countryside;
any refuge from the future;
any village that would let us live, if we could get to it.

　　Fit for love or nothing,
sometimes I slept all day for weeks on end.
Some weeks I cleaned house all night.
Some days I took myself in hand
and tore myself apart.
　　It seemed that moods, taken far enough, include their contraries.
　　If struggle's end was peace, then down the interstate,
there might be a haven from the city, and from the past:
　　A village, with dogs and berry patches, granaries and cottages,
exotic in its innocence, invisible from roads,
and, except to those living in it, nonexistent.

We waited: for the wind, or anything to bring from anywhere
the sensuousness of the simple. Every morning's rush,
with its idlings and revvings up, spoke our hopes and our hesitations.
    We kept waiting: for summer, or whatever else
might answer resignation with reprieve.
    Suddenly, we saw that all we'd waited for, though not in easy reach,
lay straight ahead, in a clearing that we entered with no confidence.
    It transfigured us.
    A pair of threatened cranes lighting on a hidden spring,
we'd found our sanctuary, and established there an independent village
consisting of the love we had begun, in which we'd stayed.

    We doubted we could stay for long, though people in the neighborhood
tell us time has time for everything.
    They teach us to steal honey
from under rocks and rafters.
Is it wrong to hope to stay or merely foolish?
    You'll be leaning out of the window, a firefly on your palm,
and I'll be happy I can thank you for all kindness, all intelligence;
for taking me out of my hands and making me happy;
and for my love, though it's in flux
from substance to illusion, memory to wish, need to happiness and back.
When love pulls extremes together, contradictions vanish.

    Nothing here exists but for us, until we live it.
A pair of long-term transients, doting old villagers, we walk
in an accord with time that makes time unimportant.
    Luxury! Such simple things create it: the air here
where earth and heaven take it easy on us.

Some snowy day, when the ground
that can move beneath us
is the same, pale gray blur as the sky that moves above,
we'll lay claim to both of them, meeting each halfway
in this *ville fortifiée,* a fragile fortress
that gives as much shelter from the future and the past
as happiness can.

Savages Taught Me

Einstein recalled: "How naive we were . . . ! Neither of us realized how much more powerful is instinct compared to intelligence."
— Ronald W. Clark, *Einstein: The Life and Times*

Savages have taught me how to catch blue starlings,
how to sleep in a deer's skin
and stroke the bear who stares at me.
　　I can't believe I'm back in the jungle.

　　I could pass for myself in the city,
eat beef with you, make allies, brag: "Look at all I have!"
Then, once again, I could meet the expectation that I'll fail.

　　Why blame myself for rotten luck?
　　You tell me that's what swooped down and sucked up
the geraniums on my patio,
the roof, bedspreads, furniture, the house, the patio, me.

　　I used to tell the world every day that I adored it.
That happiness became my misery.
I don't think I'd make it through
this wilderness of hunger, separation, longing,
if I hadn't met the little band of languageless, unclad adolescents,
greedy-eyed and offering local edibles.

　　You like tame people. Though you haven't minded
the large, wild emotions that I give, live on, question:

Who needs them—these primitive, involuntary feelings
that can be so troublesome?
    Here, I've noticed insects feed on plants
whose poisons they have overcome;
papaya trees suck their own papayas—
if foxes haven't stolen them—
to stay alive in dry times;
bucks eat grass and lions eat bucks; a tigress plucks
a peahen. Whatever fills the inner pit.
    I've tried to make desire, escape, and struggle
poetic and complex, but I'm living
because it feels good to live.

    On rainy days, I wonder if you're hungry.
I picture you outdoors somewhere, smelling of leaves,
asleep on the ground, or running in circles from pain.
I'm calling, "Baby. Baby. It's me."
    There's nobody else in my life,
though I believe my savages still follow me,
guide my hand invisibly each time I tap a tree
or reach for anything. They give me little kicks
when I show no eagerness over what I get.

    They'd have me feel all my feelings,
learn the range and stamina of warm-blooded creatures.
    It's tough to be an animal.
The wind's the devil here, and when that black rain rushes in,
the beasts must stop feeding
and run, jump, fly for all they're worth.

Soon, I'll return to the abstractions and illusions
that nourish the civilized.

City doves will cluck, showing off their mastery of defeat.
If I behave, may I stroke the place between your eyes,
the hurt spot on your heel?
I'll let you taste the flesh of one who loves even hunger.

The Uncontrollability of Things

The city moves so fast I have to race to catch you in the crowd.
My emotions, which have been in order, overflow. Certain things
can't be controlled. All the same, I pray: "No rain."
    It drizzles all April, but you march, lead protest rallies.
The crowd has a tiny mind and big complaints:
it wraps its legs around you, licks your neck, and kisses your rear end.

    Suddenly the rain pulls out the stops. Clouds drop, break us up.
In the port, immigrants are rocking in canoes;
in the suburbs, armed vets are waiting for the Japs;
in the projects, gangs of girls shoot up with melted cheese.
Terror's here. You'll be mugged by a preteen—
if the flood doesn't get you first.

    August. The sun piles up. Cars go faster out of faith.
Things appear more ordered than we thought.
Elections will be honest from now on, and every citizen
will learn to play an instrument.
The markets zoom; a football tumbles through the steely blue;
you run with it; I run with you.

    We aren't really civilized. Things—
incompetence of leaders, popular delusions, stupidity, desire—
get inside our systems, drive us crazy.
    In October, streams of cars career off cliffs while corpses
of arriving refugees drift to the docks, and you and I
use all our strength to blame and beat each other.

You're no longer hot; you're an old dissenter often asked
to leave the premises. Your speeches have all turned on you, disputing
dates of composition. Fans, camped on your front lawn, await their chance
to lick your arm skin off its bones and feed your fingers to their pets. A bomb
lobs through the battered blue, twisting TV aerials and highway overpasses.
A month of fallout and black rain, then everyone turns back to you.

But you're nobody's ace in the hole anymore, and not all storms blow over.
There's nothing to do but interview the wounded passersby,
elicit their inspiring themes: "Speech is disobedience"; "Free will has a wild beat."
Every citizen has his say, his two minutes in the sun.
The voices overlap, blend, interfere, collapse. Everyone exerts his force
on everyone, then hops into a car and drives off in all directions.

Don't ask anybody what causes what; the answers aren't safe,
are full of underestimation. Whole crowds, jaywalking right now,
may soon become the accidents we're aching for.
In the extended truce of this December,
I'm content to dangle in the light around your mouth
and beg the overwhelming heavens,
"Shine on us. Or go ahead and rain."

The Logic of Opposites

*The leaves are falling, falling as if from far up
as if orchards were dying high in space.
Each leaf falls as if it were motioning, "No."*
— Rilke, "Autumn"

Serbia is on my back; Waco was my failure.
And Birmingham, Hiroshima, Belfast: I'm implicated
in the world's disgraces. Every mood is in me, every feeling.

Chain reactions blow up laboratories, cities.
When they take place in my head, they tip my balance.
Like someone plunging from a height, I fill with terror,
with "What did I do wrong?" with "Make this not be happening,"
with "Let me out of life's vicious double-crossing trick."
I fall. I beg my bones, "Get ready not to break!"
I want to play touch football in your yard again.

Let's see what links events and moods
and why I'm always drawn into catastrophe scenarios.
I miss happiness.
I want this graveyard spiral over with, the future rolling,
our clothes flying off again, and no more images
of leg-bits and exposed bones.

You don't think up and down have much in common.
You tell me one can only fall so far, can ascend to any height.
You send fragile capsules full of delicate machinery
into space, sure you'll catch them later.

I'm imagining black holes, poisoned oceans, fallout from precision bombs.
    I'd rather have your lab coat, your van, your house, your crabapples,
your Hefty bag of dead grass, dandelions, dog droppings.
Mostly, I want *you* to have another piece of my mind:
    To look into your eyes is a suicidal leap.
Your ideas confuse me, mix and don't mix with my own.
I can't love, can't not love you, can't not blame, can't blame you,
can't stand not to understand one thing
on my way down.

    There has to be another mood.
If I'm tough on life, it's just that I'm attached to it.
    Though I've never asked for the heights of happiness,
I'll pray for a miraculous recovery.
    Maybe I can breathe differently, raise my head.
If my eyes weren't ashamed of the light falling into them,
I could go running with your Labradors again.

    The sun has reached its nadir.
Now the days will gain upon the nights:
It's the logic of things in opposition.
    I want to fall in love with you again, lie down upon
whatever has accumulated in soft heaps beneath us:
goosedown, fallen leaves, failures, errors, and illusions.
Take my hands. Uncertain of their chances, I'm extending them to you.

    At times, things settle into place.
I reached for the sun at noon; a tenth of a watt
lit sweetly on my fingertip.

Let's study frailty:
tiny flies in our wine; girls who slip from ramps at beauty pageants;
intellectuals forced out of Shanghai's windows;
Lebanon; South Africa; Sudan.

Computers gently parachute to Venus. I'm on my feet,
noticing the shaft of light that's holding up the room.

Asking for More

Raised on the uncanny, from the Gospels to remote control,
I've been amazed, but not enough.

For years, I woke to any noise, in hopes a Russian circus
had come to pitch its tent.
Then, when a stranger finally knocked, I wanted to pretend I hadn't heard.
　　Some blackness slipped in with him, but the moon moved to the window
and dangled there like a giant watch.
Even the sycamores were transfixed;
I thought I'd metamorphose into an ivory doe.

With imagination, I could measure us against immeasurable things:
shapes and speeds of nebulae; interpenetrations of the space and time
dimensions.
　　I could see his loveliness increasing with my love for him,
a love approaching sacredness without growing out of reach.
　　I shut my eyes and tried to smell a lily, tried to prove
the ancient thought that thought can grasp reality.

When he'd vanished into common daylight,
I couldn't hold before me any feature of his face:
not his swan-wing brows, not his mouth's parentheses.
　　Was my mind too open? I'd close it.
I'd concentrate on simple things: the socks he wore; the milk we drank.
Why picture him in an onyx Cougar driving along at the speed of light?

If I could let my fantasies diminish
with my love of the fantastic, I could love
what was left, be the doe who reaccepts
her solitary human form.

Why did I still see myself
strolling through a gate that swings both ways
and into iridescent blurs of dovelike shapes invisibly suspended
and shot through with calliope refrains?
    It's not that real landscapes aren't enchanting,
with their stadiums and Ferris wheels, their black and white six-lane turnpikes
flaring into cloverleaves and overpasses—
    But the dead are buried there, while the living head for distant borders.
    And it gets later all the time there.
    And the loss, the longing, then more loss, more longing
can only mean we never have enough.

With imagination, there's more shape, more limitation, more reality.

I'm asking for no less
than to summon to my mind
the scent of citrus he brought in,
the view of Jerusalem from the road to Jericho,
the way a lake feels, as it vanishes each night into the blackness,
or starlight, when it's bent by gravity.

Heaven's Extravagance

I like revelations: nametags;
banner slogans; weathermen's predictions
of how the clouds will act around Chicago.

I told myself, "Hold back,"
then gave myself away.
    I heated up some love talk till it glowed, till it glittered
in his face, made him golden.

He avoided words like "intensity," "vertigo";
threw in a few that bit: "hesitant," "indifferent";
and some that I could see right through: "light
is an extravagance of heaven," to an illusion with some truth:
"light is the extravagance of heaven."
    Night and day brilliantly exchanged their differences.
I sat in movies reading by the sunny scenes.
Chicago's lit-up skyline outdid the flamboyance overhead.
    I knew that the intensity of all the lights
was, in part, a property of brightness,
and, in part, a product of the mind.
    Some minds put out more of it—a dubious accomplishment.

When the cloud rims lost their luster for him,
his words began to shift, dissatisfied.
He wouldn't see a safety pin through my eyes.
    When a cinder from his heart made me burn, I scooped a spark
from my breast and flung it back at him.

So we both became thick smoke, while the stars
flamed above us, far away and seeming to be winking amiably.

It wasn't just moonlight that had made him shine, it was my mind,
and my mind was giving up its love of spectacles.

Better board up heaven for a while: nothing there
will tell what's going to happen, or when or why
light will turn to fire.

I didn't give up thinking.

Reading by a basement bulb,
I knew that anyone who could be dazzled
was on to something big:

Just enough intensity may be a bit too much,
but thank heaven for the gift.

For each glimmer of awareness, occurring anywhere.

And for every form of light, falling day and night
into apples, vodka, roller skates, harpsichords, and sapphires,
and upon Chicago's high-rise windows, blinding them with glare
while it shines up all her surfaces. Thank heaven for the light
that closes eyes. And opens them. And blazes all around the world
with so much love the world is crazy for it.

Hell and Up

In imaginary plays starring those I love and hate,
tragedy brings comedy, which summons up dejection, which becomes
elation, which turns to misery.
    Extremes have their appeal:
go the limit, then reverse.
    Mirroring the universe, I swing:
high to low, fast to slow, supernova dazzle
to black-hole black.

    Today the arc of my trapeze is taking me Downtown.
Downtown, Uptown's "Over There."
Uptown, Downtown's "Over There."
Uptown's locked in overdrive.
Downtown's sunk in dead despair.

    Downtown, from 6:00 to 8:00 P.M., I gathered up my bones, getting over
1:00 to 5:00 P.M., when I scooped out my marrow, making up for
1:00 to 5:00 A.M., which I spent listening to my blood
complain to me of me.
    It hates me, like you and me and everything I love (FALSE):
the sky, my eyes, my favorite FM station, and the jazz it's sending up
that's really war. (FALSE.)
    But here's a PLUS: a song by Steely Dan
that I can weigh against my MINUSES—
like the time you tried to murder me. (FALSE.)

Hearing those two guys do "East St. Louis Toodle-oo"
makes me tough enough (TRUE)
to modify my charge against you, Common Thief (FALSE).

• • •

My next apparatus has a trick-to-death mechanism.
Gently up the roller coaster slope I go. Careening down,
I pick up speed; six G's of me push through me.

Meanwhile, you've switched the radio to AM and tuned in the news:
The NASDAQ climbs sky-high; a helicopter in Iraq
is hit by friendly fire; Burt Lancaster of Alcatraz is dead;
six are gunned down in the New York subway. The tired, two-party system
drags its feet, while a fresh airplane crash
moves up there with the country's top disasters.
Hate and love! Many giant MINUSES. Here and there, a tiny PLUS.

I'm revolving in the teardrop loop, where costly horror
alternates with cut-rate joy.
I don't mean much when I scream—
only that the section of my brain reserved for pain has swollen, overflowing
on the sector set aside for panic, which spills
onto the area designed for agony, which infects
the sanity compartment.
I'm concentrating on the tap of raindrops on the roof,
when I see it isn't rain; it's pieces of my skin,
flying off me at the walls. (FALSE.)
After this, screaming has real meaning. (TRUE.)

Turn that radio down, Home Intruder. I can't share
your love for *All Things Considered* now. Or spin the dial from NPR,
find us something relevant, and turn the volume up:
    Menuhin's violin might bring some useful fantasy (I'll be fine),
or one truth that just might mean *life* has meaning (I'll be fine).

• • •

    I labor up the next incline of my mood machine.
    If I can keep my enemies—my blood electrolytes—in line,
and my friends—my blood electrolytes—in line,
I won't have to plunge this time, losing, all at once, my hard-won gains.
    I'm on top. Hold me, Prince of Con Men.
    You're on top. We meet the G's.
    In your arms, I gladly give up gravity, which, after half an hour
of elevation, you give back to me.
    I get back my thoughts, no longer false,
my flesh no longer hateful to itself.
    After that, I have to weep that I can't hoard my bliss,
can't contain my love,
that always was beyond beyond.

• • •

    In your hands, I can grasp the opposites.
Or I should say I see how they grip me.
    Each extreme, so incomplete alone as to be wrong,
delineates, extends, begins to set the other right.
    I start my trips to heaven from a pit.

I'm fine; I'm rocking gently at mid–Ferris wheel.
The universe oscillates between Big Bang and Big Collapse.
If I'm headed Over There again, my Radio Darling,
I'll have the laws of motion and mechanics at my side.

Let's have music! News!
I won't give up studying amusement park contraptions
that go up to the top where love spills over
from down at the bottom where the love comes from.

Designing Heaven

The Bible never really describes heaven.
I'd put the plains of Africa in mine:
Flocks of marabou, high-stepping through papyrus fans;
a herd of lyre-horned topi; Masai elders in red blankets
sitting on the amber hills.
And women walking single file, as I've seen them do,
washtubs full of kindling on their heads.
It's not clothes that make those women beautiful.

Watch. A woman pauses in her repetitious work
to massage, with her fingertips, cream into her skin.
She goes in circles. Still,
she's the calm Center, with an inner cycle
synchronized with the moon's and with the other womens'.
Her hips are draped with babies, and with sarongs
dyed russet, copper, beautiful with chicory, sumac, walnut hulls.
Unwrapped, she's much more beautiful.

I hadn't been on friendly terms with harmony:
the march-in-step through school, the family romance.
Oh I saw the beauty of neutral shades, basic rules.
But it was fuchsia and chartreuse—the wilder colors—
that I loved. And unfixed forms—trapezoids and habitats
and stars that leave sphericity behind
as if preferring just to blur
and radiate from one shape to another.

Protruding from the gray Zambesi River:
hippopotamus nostrils. All at once, the head's up;
then the dripping hippo waddles onto shore;
a red sac slides from her back half, slips to the grass.
A pink nose pokes a hole into the crimson membrane;
soon, a baby hippo's pushing through.
      Clambering up the riverbank, eight more hippopotami
encircle Mother and her newborn with ecstatic mooing.

      I hadn't given symmetry its due.
Repetition was inevitable; why call it beautiful?
But how perfect, that circle, completed
by each hippopotamus on its perimeter. Call it beautiful.
The double helices of DNA: beautiful.
Space, with her cycles of expansion and contraction: beautiful.
      Anyone can see, for efficient navigation of the heavens,
celestial bodies have to be spherical; beautiful.

      Tanzania's animals aren't any more rambunctious
than subatomic particles:
forms forming patterns too exquisite
to identify as anything but exquisite patterns.
      Watch. Wildebeest and zebra, old companions,
make a ring of transfixed silhouettes around a cheetah
killing a gazelle.
The whole famished landscape's watching, too:

      The cheetah eats.
      Her jaws scissor, whiskers glitter.
      With her teeth, she dangles an intestine
above the dead tommy's pretty face,

then plucks and sets aside her prize,
the pulpy, rosy stomach: a mango at the center
of the never-still life
rearranging itself upon the plain.

I've found Paradise in earth-tones,
watched copper-colored women work red and yellow corn
out of orange clay
and tabby lions and triple stars
gather, scatter, skid around:
inhabitants of heaven,
beautifully loose
among the rules that call them beautiful.

For Dear Life

We thought we would be at sea for three days at most.
— Pedro Gamez

Before we pushed off for Moon in Mañana Land,
we watched the rain from twig-and-blanket tents on Cuba's beaches.
Hundreds of empty rafts rose and fell in the azure swell.
One by one, they heaved off, overloaded,
and were swallowed up by the curve of the earth.
    Some who sailed came floating back, mud in their mouths,
fish in their trousers, and moving their eyes as if alive.
    What a way of Nowhere! As if a raft with a mast

could improve our agony!
    I'd thought we were all relatives.
We had gods for the helpless, since there was no help for them,
also no medicine, work, or money, only the hungry
to feed the hungry, and the too-common, honorable desperation.
    When we fell on the picked remains of a pig some outsider had stolen,
we called that outcast one of us,
the theft legitimate.

An ocean away from Florida, even walking isn't free.
    The sun is twenty feet above me; sharks are circling, close enough
to watch my chest steaming sweat, my eyes leaking ocean.
    We're lost beneath a sky that birds can figure and divide.

Milk finished, we begin to signal with our shirts and buckles.
It's no help to gnaw my lips; I'm about to drink this sea
I'm tossed upon, that makes me wonder
why life would start in it.

How we've waited to be welcome! Starving,
we bound down the gangplank. They ask who we are that we're starving,
then march us back up to go elsewhere.
Where? Oh God! It's Nowhere!
Guantánamo, Cuba, a refugee camp with khaki tents, a video store,
a laundromat, razor wire, Cuban music blasting night and day,
and little water. They call it "Paradise." We have to pray
they let us die right here for the rest of our lives.

In disbelief they'd sail for nothing,
and in faith the world awaits them,
boats are loading now in China. Don't they hear *us*, shouting "Miami!"?
I won't wrap *my* skin around their disembarking skeletons.
I want to tell America the Beautiful my *own* raft stories:
how the ocean, riled at being second-guessed,
chewed my hopes and spit them in my face mixed with vomit
no wind would take away;

how thirst turned to pain;
how each of us bled and prayed only for himself,
held on for dear life or whatever it would take
to get out of it, or get let in at last.
So here we are, holding on by anger, hunger, wonder that we're still
holding on, having crossed an ugly gulf to be back as we began:
scavenging—though it's *our* bones that have been sucked of marrow—
hoping

we won't be combing Nowhere for those bones
before the degradation's over.

    Now and then, we catch them hating us; they catch us holding
everything they own against them. It's not fate; it just happens.
One lacks; the other clutches. One pulls back;
the other clings.

    We have no choice in that: we're still here, here, here
in this mess of a sea that never settles.

When It Was Your World

Born and promptly raised, you went to school with two black eyes,
fit right in.
Nothing but your magic tricks had happened,
but you knew there was a world. You wanted to join up.
You'd have ridden the sea in a box.

Unable to invent the other hemisphere, you were surprised by China,
her suspension bridges, reservoirs, and motherlodes of every one
a famished land might need.
In Beijing, you sat on curbs with girls with white-slave smiles
and boys who looked like Buddha. Keeping your ascetic rule—love everybody—
you infused them with your power and charisma.
(How good that you know everyone the minute that you meet!)

The world was yours. You only had to undermine authority
and choreograph the crowds. Then the government jumped out,
shouting, "Shut up, Big Nose!" and offered you a job
scratching dust with a toothbrush from crevices in steps of monuments.
That's when you became a people's actor,
found and faced your light. In confidential tones,
you told women peddling breast milk, men playing Go in the road,
"I know everything." You got big, bigger, filled auditoriums.

The audience started making silly faces in your face,
but the thrill of "fight" in the alligator portion of your brain
became the happy thought of how posterity would honor you.

Suddenly the gods fell out, declined to send more rain
or any clue how to rescue a gigantic country
with no gasoline, no power lines, your six-yard cotton allotment,
a million golden images of Buddha, little money,
and everyone denouncing you for trying to rule the world.

They were ready for another candidate.
Arrested for protesting, you didn't even get top prison billing.
After your release, the government, with your cooperation,
rewrote history. (Everyone should clarify his thinking now and then.)
Every mouthful tasted of defeat. You still believed
you should have been the one to teach the poets
to electrify the countryside.

Children still managed to be born.
(Everyone does something brutal sometimes.)
Fights you'd started got along without you.
What about the course of history?
You'd brought the women to their windows,
gathered up the smiles of Shanghai.
From now on, the bicyclists on Nanjing Road
were on their own.

Back home, in a dominion too tiny for a name,
you've shut yourself away with your piano and red chair.
You're ambitious for the stars and birds.
Who'd choose to rule a world that throws everybody out?
Those boys upon whom spring made no impression,
the men who rose through the ranks,

those who spoke out loudly and were wrong,
those who dreamed of kitchen chores:
what heroes you've become!

Care for them. Bring no battles here.
You'll still suffer like a soldier, maybe find
a little spot in eternity
above some foreign city
and drink your fill of the blare and cancan of humanity
in a universe where suns are born and worlds created every day.

To Be a Different Person

Left to myself, as I nearly always am,
I think I'll change my nose, name, fingerprints.
To be a different person.
　　Maybe it's not me who thinks, but another self
who's Chinese or Jewish. Or a waitress named Sam.
　　"Hi, Sam. I'll have everything."
　　Looking in the mirror after a bath
for some confirmation of a simple "I am,"
my breath clouds my face and then the rest of me.
Do other people disappear before their eyes?

　　I wasn't anyone's idea. I had no calling, either.
　　I had regrets for everything I did
and ten years of consoling fantasies growing in me.
I put on a good face and acted like my heroes, not so much
because I wanted to achieve anything, but just to be a different person.
　~ My family was puzzled when I spoke about myself as "she":
"At night she puts tomorrow's clothes upon the chair and shapes them like a girl,
then she slips out of her skin, sheds her face and failures, leaves her memories
in the bedroom, and becomes a different person someplace else.
She doesn't want to have another thought about herself."

　　One winter I was Lincoln, Proust, and Fred Astaire,
one month each. How I—Fred—bamboozled them
about my hands, too big for a dancer:
I hid the middle fingers underneath the outer ones.

I never did those those double jetés—the old self resisted. But sometimes, in "Something's Got to Give," I'd hear myself whisper, "Now you're dancing."

In lobbies full of runaways who'd ducked in from the everlasting outside, someone would speak to me in English. I'd reply in French.
If he switched to French, I'd do the old Soft Shoe and croon,
"Somebody's got to dance with Leslie Caron."

I thought about myself this morning, realized
it's been a while since I've been stupefying.

Medication takes away the other selves.

That seven-volume masterpiece that clasps memory to its breast
was not my composition after all.

Nor were the mutton chops that camouflaged my bony face
my mutton chops. That girl who wore my clothes and whined,
"I'm having a bad dream," I tricked her
and she disappeared. As for the relatives, I got them back
with an personal ad: "All's forgiven. No hard feelings."

Speaking to myself in the second person:
So you'd still like to take a nap, wake up in 1936
and prevent a famous crime? You've earned a few grand thoughts
for all of your self-sacrifice. Why not pretend instead
that your many times around the block have left no mark on you?
That it's the same old yellow summer moon over pines that grow
so close to the blacktop, you can't escape the sweetness of them.

Balzac, on his deathbed, called out for his characters.

There's another way to welcome runaways: the door, half-open
between the life composed of dreams and the life that's getting lived.

Until it's irresistible, don't even think of sleep:
you've got real possiblities!

The Outback

All day I try to shake off thoughts that fall away at night:
in the unconscious, I have what I want.
It's the only continent where everything that's happened
can happen, but it may be
more of what I want than I wanted.
    He grows still; I grow still beside him. In sleep, we separate
and go where we're not separated.
    Coffee fields, copper mines, and coconut groves cross my mind,
replacing other thoughts. I'm in the outback of Down Under,
its mist-heavy forests, its neolithic hills and plains.

    Here, grotesque marsupials are beautifully asleep
in a blue confusion of eucalyptus trees.
There are bandicoots, rock wallabies, koalas.
Egrets shelter in palmettos, and, in a billabong,
a large orange starfish is standing on one arm.
    An immobile wombat starts to eat,
then sucks up bugs and leaves in incorrigible gluttony.
I see myself caught in a vine and chew my leg off to get free.
I leap, snatch, howl, and swing between exquisite greed

and panicky retreat from the forest—the dream. But consciousness,
with its interpretations, also disconcerts. I plunge down under once again:
    Kangaroo are bounding in ecstatic pairs toward a waterhole.
    They stop short: jackal may be waiting in the fuchsia bougainvillea.
Each large and little roo, the rabbit, rat-toed, and the musk roo
must approach alone. I'm with them in eagerness, then terror, then relief

that it's only an old hippo, rising like a question mark from the reservoir,
carrying upon his back our old grandfather clock.

Crushing larkspur, artichoke, and fennel underneath their hooves,
the kangaroo depart through the jacaranda violets and yellow candle-bush:

more outback, alive with emu, platypus, and any two
of anything who choose to be together, or any one who can be still alone.

Half-awake, I touch the man of whose flesh I know so little
and in which I am so lost. Animals must live in him: he's never still
within me. In urgency and innocence at 5 o'clock a.m.,
then in the stillness that does come, we're not separated.

Later, in the forest within the outback woods, a couple of Tasmanian
wolves
lick and scratch, sniff and mount in their shingle house. They growl, claw, mount
again,
then sleep through the aggressions and arousals of their dreams.

I wake up open-mouthed, tantalized by flying images,
grasping at the colors I'd recovered in the dark.

A silky paw is slipping through my palm. Next to me,
my husband's sleeping. I grow still again,
knowing what I want:
not to master it, that outback, with its springs and jungles,
but to let it stay unbeaten.

The Substance of Evanescent Things

Being a romantic is my calling: I ache
for victories over time and space.

He said, "Come close. You'll soon be warm."
We kissed; I ran to the window panting;
he ran after me; my blood sang.
I became cooperative, ready to climb on to him
and be transported.

"Stand there. I want to stare at you."
He asked for everything, offering little more
than the fever patches on his cheeks,
his chest with "Dominance" inscribed upon it.
I wanted something, too:
to enfold him in that room where we never watched our language.
He confided in me with his arms and legs.
I pressed my mouth upon his neck,
filled my head with his essence,
watched the room go out of focus, let myself be lifted
to a sweetness with a self-erasing quality
that asked to be repeated. Was it a rush,
a splurge, a charge? It left no evidence.

But there were facts: he had fair skin,
a touching hardness to his bones, a ragged scar
across one shoulder, an attachment to his limbs,
and a face on which he'd written half his story.

There were facts formed by sensations: time was told
by physical changes; happiness was made of pleasures
as short-lived as happiness.

He was taking something from my breast, leaving nothing
but impressions of his hands. But his hands
had much to do with my formation. I began
committing him to memory, preparing for a future when I'd sit
and make him nonmysterious.

Time was up.

Sometimes I imagine him as he exists without me:
he stands with an odd forward slant,
as if the floor were sloping away.

I want him only with my eyes.

My hands, mouth, labyrinth
aren't involved at all.

He may be halfway to Antigua
or living under an alias in a distant city.
Our romance is more mine than his, though it's from him
I learned the weight of memory, time, sensation.

I'm through with fantasy.
The space he takes up in me
is one fact no one can say I dreamed.

We Could Swim in It

Chiffon curtains blow into the bungalow
bringing hints of ocean.
I like the water close, though I already know
too much about waves and undertow.

The sea got to me early; I could lose my thoughts in it.
It's gotten darker lately, and the blue clouds loose around it
crowd the sky. I can't make out where air gives way to water.
At night, dust and light get more confused then ever.
The wind swings away, then the oleanders sink
through a display of shades of green
too deep to distinguish.
On his long haul from nowhere to anywhere,
a hitchhiker's running to a ride.

One thought of him makes the dark go out of focus;
my breath holds itself. He wasn't anyone
I knew, but loving anyone
deepens, displaces, implicates one
in the worldwide longing.
At first, my soul went into a crescendo.
The air couldn't stop kissing me.
Now I'm floundering in depth,
but it's still me drowning, isn't it?

I close my eyes as soon as I wake up, lie in bed till noon,
pull the shades after lunch and lie two hours longer.

My lips move constantly, silently recounting:
    "I licked the salt from his skin. We were on the water.
All we saw was shimmer. We could swim in it . . ."
    No fact is not misleading.
No flash of wing or fin brings any wisdom.
The catamarans stranded on the beach
are a revelation of incompetence.

    As water is by water, I'm confused by love.
    Who can really rest upon its surface?
    Underneath, I'm passionately struggling
to shake away impressions passion left on me.
    Visions triple in my head:
dolphins caught and twisting in a tuna net;
a luxury liner rotting in the churchlike light of coral reefs,
while streams of bubbles from its hull dance upward
through the water, turning it electric blue.

    I thought I could stop touching bottom, could escape the skeletons
and swells of unspeakable emotion on the ocean floor.
Though even on its face, a breeze makes shadows I can't fathom—
I who say that waves "caress" and whitecaps "love" the wind.
    "Love" again. All the fuss about it must mean something.

    Another prisoner might have tamed a pelican.
    Working hard to breathe, here where I'm no one
to anyone but me, I've gotten sure of this:
I love this sea. It's permanent. It's here for me
to drink. It's bitter, odious.
I love it.

Part II

A dance before two armies.

— Song of Solomon 6:13

In Touching Distance

How much another person means to me
may not come in a comfortable quantity.
To have been in touching distance can create so acute a joy
it makes all the senses oversensitive.
    I'll shudder at strong colors,
taste the acid in an apricot,
then suddenly I swear I'm tasting everything in the refrigerator.
The nerves in my heels and toes start dancing;
I think my feet will shake loose from my ankles;
I understand the intimacy of happiness and pain.

    A little torture can be pleasant.
    Once, some boy poured a bucketful of sand on my head,
and my ears and eyebrows hurt
for his hairgrease, his knobby elbows, all of him.
    I thought then I'd always want to be
someone dancing, laughing, clasping,
who tells her bones and muscles to go ahead and ache,
who savors every swallow of blue sky as it slides down her throat,
who sends every form of love an open invitation
to her flesh.

    But temperaments are shaped by distress as well as pleasure.
And anyone who's overextended,
who relies upon a billion unreliable nerve endings
can develop strange conditions where sensations contradict.

Anyone who's suffered from extremity overload,
mango poisoning, sunflower fever—or who's merely had too much
sweetness sucked from her lips,
who's wept the water out of her
and believed the grass has wept when she's walked on it,
knows that when these torments stop, that's a form of bliss.

I've praised myself for all that I've avoided—
men who are brusque with waiters,
women who don't appreciate interior design,
kids, pets, cocktail parties, public gatherings.
Then one night I gave a lift
to someone standing at a four-way stop sign in a sudden shower.
When I stopped again to drop him off, I saw his face,
his blue-green jacket with the blue-green faded out,
and said I'd take him someplace else, anyplace he wanted.
I knew I was in for it.

This time, before it worked its way deeper, through the ribs,
I felt love in my hands.
In the car's little atmosphere, molecules of uncondensed rain
began to sting my palms, my wrists, the skin that webs my fingers.
I'd reached into a honeycomb, and the bees had come.

Action at a Distance

Turn out the light; see how the sky affects us.
   With your cheekbone two inches from my forehead,
tell me the mass and circumference of the universe
and how at home you are in its basic emptiness. I need
these revelations, though they sound disconsolate in your mouth.
   Aren't there plenty of planets, moons, and stars
spinning gently toward each other,
and plasma jets as incandescent as a hundred million suns
sending fire through space so it can feel something?
Don't you connect the stars to make your friends: the Ram, Orion?
   Admit that and we'll be inseparable.

   My right foot barely brushes your left ankle;
I could spend a pleasant hour guessing cloud dimensions.
   If the earth that moves below is no more ours
than everything that moves above, don't say it. Don't tell me
that our yellow-apple moon can steal the daylight,
leaving, where the sun had shone, an onyx disc
shivering with starquakes, clanging like a gong,
making roses fold, chickens roost, roosters go hysterical.
You think only you have turned away from an eclipse?
   Call it "action at a distance." Let's rename everything
in honor of our happiness and exclusivity.

   Two people have surprises for each other. I thought
we were long past the passion/madness point, and only had
to fill the space. But all we have between us are these two adjacent bodies

and a sky too big to see. We keep turning. What's come up?
A shining, unexpected paragraph? An alien phrase
just made to separate us? Whether we are turning from
what's much too difficult—some ancient ache, returning
to tamper with the universe—or facing off over what
was merely difficult, we see how solitarily we turn.

　　And even in the amber atmosphere of electricity, the loveliest
discovery since the kiss, there are times when we can't see each other.

　　I won't tell you now the earth is flat and simple.
　　I have some words, hoarded from our hours of harmony.
We'll go past "love," with what it wasn't, straight to "love."
　　Ask anyone: a skyful of white ibis,
flying off, half north, half south, to see what moves them
finds the sky. Can't lose it.
　　Look up: double stars
navigate a blackness
too distant and exquisite to explain us to ourselves.
　　Will we ever fathom it?
Is there enough in space to outweigh the loneliness?

Apologia

Maybe my old boyfriends shouldn't read this.
They complain about me now; if they learn more, they might boycott me.
I used to say to them, "If I could choose, would I cruise town
honking my horn at nothing like you do? Hell, no! I'd bust my ass
and become an exotic dancer! I'd disappear from stage
just before I'd stripped completely."

I rode the bus for years to get here, fifteen miles from home,
beneath the Ferris wheel of a fair too broke to leave Old Gulf, Mississippi.
I put myself through beauty school: Bardot, Garbo, and Colette.
I play an instrument: I sing. I do "My Way" in a G-string
with a tuft of marabou.
Clara Barton, Little Darla, Betty Ford: I've been them.

The character's not in the clothes. It's in the pivot, kick, and glide
for my audience of former beaux. I'm still their girl.
They remember me at the Dairy Queen in 1968, peeling
out of a yellow slicker, somehow pulling out of my sleeve
an intact banana split. The truth is, I was practically a virgin—
as they found out when they tried to get let in.

These boys have naughty thoughts. They grew up where every boy
is every boy's buddy; lived on novels where somebody did the things
they wanted to; taught Romance languages; indexed their anthologies:
"The Chase"; "Conquest"; "Evasion."
They say I talk like a Yankee now. They sound the same: "More."
Why am I the one who says, "I'm sorry"?

And when I step into my light before them, why do I think
I'm back in their back seats, yelling, "Let me out!"?
    I can't take this carousel music. I can't tell applause from rain.
Fan mail keeps me going, but mixed with it, I get
attacks from critics: "Clean up the act or offer extra services!"
What happened to the dance analysts? It's the sex thing, isn't it?

    I'd take the whole gallery of old boys into my dressing room,
and make more apologies: "I'm deep in an aesthetic of extremes."
And "I'm a contradiction, with my T. and A., my ballerina's attitudes.
    "My story's basically *Anna Karenina*, only with a stripper:
I got taken to the fair and distracted at the skeet-shoot booth
while I got tattooed behind my back."

    The boys could tell their stories, too; I'd grow more accessible:
    "Look! Scars, darlings! This one, down my inner thigh, is 'Lost on you.'
That one, from the bellybutton up, is called 'You got me!'
    "You love the female body, but everyone's of two minds about sex.
    "Don't mess with the sitting duck etched upon my bottom.
Think about Astaire and Rogers: women spin for gentlemen."

    The music will go round and round, and soon, in the mirror,
I'll find another character in lurex thong and tassels,
with a bit of Emma Bovary's bliss to dignify her passions.
    But first, the swivel. See?
    The trick's not in the hips, but in the knees. And there's more:
the bump, grind, shimmy, strut.
    When I demonstrate them to my buddies, we'll agree
there aren't that many easy steps for any of us.

Inside Job

One self goes out, painfully; the other stays
painfully suppressed. The hidden self
has the upper hand, since she's crazy.

She thinks "anyone" stands for "everyone."
She collects all the little kicks she gets,
and if they amount to something, comes undone.
Blaming *me* for this, of all people,
she takes my lungs and lips and screams,
"Drop dead, Idiot!"

In Junction Springs, a turnaround on an Alabama road,
no one had a choice but to be family.
Each was scorned by someone, and forgiven for it.
I was simple then: I could hardly
keep myself from telling everyone, "You're a part of me."
Contractors who came home drunk and sobered up
in backhouses; checkout girls; umpires; bums,
consoling and in need of consolation, like everyone:
I felt so much for them, I almost thought I *was* them.

I didn't know the public was a thug—
a guy-on-the-sidewalk type who likes to yell "Shut up!"
The female public, subtler, hates the female face.
I never wore see-thru blouses, never went to amusement parks,
got a prize for Latin Elegaics

and a bad reputation, even in the family:
they thought my laughing frenzies and uncontrolled devotions
meant that I was antisocial.

   One of my sisters crashed the Ford.
Another rode her motorcycle into someone's Oldsmobile.
   Everybody got home in one piece, but The Insider had come out
and was hissing at me, "All your fault, Moron!"
   I totaled Mamma's Volkswagen. By then, half my sisters
suspected I was out to wreck the family. How could they know
that The Old Girl, who outwept everyone
as we watched the evening news, was a home intruder?

   It's time someone got through to her. I can sing her tune:
   "Dummy, *you* shut up!
Bang your head against my bones. Sleep."

   I want to watch the wars in peace,
though television's images
don't contain the ravaged souls
who shatter me, and whom I'd mend.

   That includes you, Sister, who can't see benevolence
until it kicks you in the teeth.
   You split from me so I could be
taken in by other people, so that you
could wear my scars and on your sleeve, part of my heart,
broken by the old ungainly love that opened it.

Get yourself together now.

Let the mind that made you be your haven.

Go back through the maze you've made

of my brain with all your thinking.

Sink, sink, sink

into that fascinated, dazed, defective apparatus.

Get lost. Then I'll reclaim

unmitigated love for every messed-up, broken-down,

blood-and-flesh contrivance: every blessèd one

who tears at me; clings to me; makes me weep from fury,

pity, misery, frustration; wrecks my sleep.

Pick Up the Pieces

The emergency workers of Iowa were helpless
when the Mississippi swelled one night from ten feet to a mile across,
flooding kitchens, cornfields, Des Moines, and Davenport,
picking up ducks, hats, cows in Quincy, houses in St. Louis,
tossing them around as it tore down-country.
    Trouble's in us, too. In you and me and anyone
with passion that's become too much for him.
    Love's dialogue turns argument,
and anyone can be caught short.

    A small-town southerner, I longed for a square dance in Chicago
so you, Captain of Commerce, could promenade with me.
I might as well have wanted to run for governor.
    We were opposites, intoxicated, troubled:
you called me "Broad," I called you "Brat"
(in any dance, there's some antagonism).
Our fantasies were anxious, slapstick, trivial, and tragic:
each day we unwished the last, then woke up early
hurrying the next.

    Trouble hit Homestead, Baton Rouge, Charleston;
people stood in lines not knowing what they'd get: whatever, they'd lost it.
    Alabama wept; New York didn't bat an eye; Texas sent a clean-up crew;
L.A. had its own bad news. In Chicago, you were smug: Just when I had been laid off,
you'd made killings for your buddies using your Insider's tips. You asked how I
could question the Commodities Exchange. I hadn't questioned anything.

I *knew* the U.S.A was suited for a Civil War. Bull Run pulled through.
Then Gettysburg—where even now, a few can fit into the boots of soldiers
whose spirits hold us, whom we hold, on pedestals, in stone and metal.

I knew why you rubbed my nose, over all my protests, in how much loot
you'd gotten for your pals: you needed my poor heart that beat for you
beneath you. But in continual defeat, could I keep what love you'd given?
Or could I hit bottom? I'd probably wind up in the Loop, with bare feet
and a sign reading "Where will you spend eternity?" And you confiding to me
your Exxon stock's gone up.
Our love-line's down. I've had enough
of Haves who give the Have-Nots little kicks. You kill me with Your Victories.
Talk about losses. Talk about conflict. Talk about trouble. Time to split.

Now maybe I can overcome my doubts about my patchwork skirt,
while you get over yours about the Common Man and holding hands
and join, just once, the honored line of peapickers, cowboys, and rodeo clowns
whose big-time troubles never touch their country nonchalance
as they stomp upon the sequined hats they once twirled and tipped.
I'll be with the girls held up by crinolines and chewing gum.
And when the lines meet in Chicago, Dallas, Pittsburgh, and Seattle,
we'll swing new partners, fling away what's useless, broken, over,
love the future, and somehow refuse to hate the past.

Savannah

It's been a while since I've seen Savannah,
with her downtown squares, her circular marshes.
    People hurry there for calm: the British debtors
Oglethorpe handpicked for second chances;
Moravians from Bohemia, Jews from Germany,
Salzburgers from Austria, and the Highland Scots.

    One fall day, I'll show my face on Gaston Street again.
My sister Janet may be sweeping sycamore balls from the steps
of a gray, colonial townhouse in the city's quiet center.
    The red persimmons dangling near the curved porch rail—
I'll want to hold them—and the lion head on the gate, the stained-glass window,
paved backyard, camellia garden, our whole block. And on the west,
Drayton Street, and on the east, Abercorn,
where I might see Michèle, Celia, Cabell, Jeanne, or Henry.

    When the winter tangerines drop to our double balcony,
let the sunlight break into component shades:
    Here, yellows harmonize with violets, and the bluejays
make their peace with silence.
    Why debate with Pamela, Cynthia, Ellen
the safety of the neighborhoods north of Broughton, south of Dancy?
Let the restorations under way in every district
tell us we'll hold on to what we've got.
    We've lost too much already:
Courtney; Roscoe; Ricky; Ben; my Rosalind.

When fishermen on Skidaway Road
say they've been ripped off
by modern carpetbaggers packing taxes from the Capitol,
I'll remind myself that Sherman didn't burn Savannah down.
He left my lighthouse, plots of peaches, Wesley Methodist,
and, in the parks, on pedestals half-buried in azaleas in the spring,
war heroes overseeing peace,
recovery, the endless Reconstruction.
I've been rehabbed myself. Daddy told me
take all the time I needed, though there wasn't much.

Mamma said whoever comes to love this cracker town
will get big enough to hold her architecture, history,
gaslights, rainspouts, fountains circled by iron lace.
And Tybee, Sandfly, Isle of Hope, Thunderbolt, Moon River;
docks, forts, cobblestones, cannons, catamarans;
Erica and Robert's house overlooking Bluff Drive;
wild gardenias, palms, magnolias, live oaks, Spanish moss.
I can almost touch
summer's mauve hydrangeas and fuchsia oleanders—they're swaying
in the heat that made their colors. I'm picking up
the thin, separate voices of my Daisy, Jackson, Ross, Kurt, and Carley
as they blend into the rich, old calm
that never holds me long enough.

The Day All Sides Claim Victory

Love is your last chance.
— Louis Aragon

Some days, they bore the daylights out of me:
lovers, sprawling on hot sand,
probably paid off by local governments
to keep up the disrepute of paradise.
    I avoid savage mainlands.
    Seabirds pump exhaustedly for any island tossed up by the sea;
wreck survivors wash in half-alive; I also fling myself
on far-flung bits of earth
no less connected than the rest of it.

    In Fiji, they never forecast weather, due to weather.
They stand on tiptoe on thatched roofs and reach for heaven.
    I hear women wailing to appease malicious spirits,
kids scavenging like cats, and the contentious squeaking
that teaches Fiji's mice to act like rats.
    With colonial misery etched into their skin, natives here
trust prevailing winds. Let those breezes ruffle up the dragon trees,
asylums for migrating butterflies for centuries. And let me love
the mighty high I'm riding, love the ledge of happiness I lie on—

until I swing to Kingston.
I take up with a cop there. He stops traffic with one arm.
Kids jump up and touch it as they cross the street.

I love the way he gives those orders; I jump, too.

He thinks I should be glad to get anything he dishes out,
sweet or rotten. He's afraid I'll grab a bit of his sugar-cane domain.
He takes me first, for all I'm worth.

I'm not innocent: on an island dominated by the poppy trade,
the poison trade, I wanted to swap hearts with him.

I beat it for Tahiti, where Captain Cook found Venus,
Captain Bligh, food for slaves. They take in anyone.

They say whatever happens here, has a right to happen.

Let Papeete's butterflies eat the sweat of sleeping bums;
let women stoop to witchcraft to win the hearts
of men who fight with bamboo, grudges, voodoo, spears, and coconuts.
Even here, everything turns weapon in a war.

That would be no skin off me if I were just a passerby.
But I sink into where I am. I'm here now. I'm implicated.

I came seeking calm, but I had battles waiting in my bones,
Sherman on his march through Georgia and the Trojan Horse
about to open in my gut: history's great brigades all set
to mobilize inside me. Only where's the Eighth Army,
the Hell on Wheels Battalion, sent over by the U.S.A.
to save the day and end all these uprisings?

There are eternal structures to defend, perhaps to topple.

There are winds doubling against rocks, and cuttlefish preparing
to overthrow the ocean.

Some guy tries not to look my way over his margarita.
He goes out, comes in, steals another glance I don't allow,
then lets me steal one back. This little tug of war
has many of us on each side, slaves

of want and weakness since the days our mouths
first sucked our mothers' breasts. Love?
Who can think of that now? But let him kiss my hair,
brush it back, kiss my face. If I drift off,
I'll tell him where I've been: "In my own kingdom."

There are pirates in the jungles of orchid islands, coral coasts.
There's black sand, white sand, green sand, butterflies so thick
on branches, branches break. There's the way that lilac blossoms
drop to spider strings, while hawkmoths visit honeysuckle.
There are ships for solace, swims among pink starfish,
and in the evenings, balances to be struck between us.
There's the heat, streaming upward.
How much love I'll need
for my heart to keep its peace.

Gold Rush: 1848/1996

The motorcycle cop was performing rodeo stunts
when I called, "That all you got?
Serving and protecting worn you out?"
   Yesterday, while Chicago's Best put on their Denver boots,
Ms. Nature kicked some lake into the Planetarium.
The lower stars got soaked.
   Today, the air is thin and gold.
   I'm in fake fur; he's in sergeant's blues.
He gets a hot dog, I make do with coffee.

   He asks if I want something else.
   Like a contestant in a beauty pageant
who can't say "baloney sandwich," I reply, "World Peace."
   Everybody comes to private terms with public eyes.
   Do I limp apologetically in tattered satin through a classy bash
when all the other partygoers sparkle loud enough
to make Miss Universe feel shabby?
   Or be glad I've got a mouth on me, and, when someone's listening,
a line or two to speak?

   While gusts begin to whip at us, I tell the cop my top secret:
I once stripped for a magazine, like starlets do for art.
I did it to be nude.
   Nobody's girl was everybody's baby after that—
for five lousy hundred bucks. Everybody's glitter-driven nitwit's what I was,
though I'd studied all the Best Plays in the language.

Now I know my destiny: no destiny. Now, of all
the tragic, comic, and romantic heroes, it's the fools I love.
Who cares who they are? They just walk on and harmonize—

nothing like the fools in the Commodities Exchange,
where we escape the gale. Here, it blusters *inside;*
with shrieks for "Wheat!" "Pork bellies!" "Gold!"
　　"Gold" can mean money, power, fame, adoration—
anything wanted more than anything.
　　It's gold that's sold in dummy corporations, counted up
in final countdowns, divvied up with Sudden Death, raked in
after questioning the Best Evangelists:
　　"Can rich, richer, richest lead to broke?"

　　At the Policemen's Ball,
I wear my good junk jewelry;
he wears his Silver Star.
　　We dance; he sings in my ear
"Heart Like a Wheel," both verses.
　　You belters-out of platinum hits,
this fellow's just as musical,
could get himself a spread at the head
of the Country and Western chart.

　　But who cares who hangs on how long to what Top Spot?
　　Let's just have some fun,
act like ladies, gentlemen,
make this gym a real theater, where no costumes hide
puny shoulders, guns and knives, puny brains,
cocaine in veins, puny souls, loaded dice,
the blindness of the Fools in all of us, and the insights.

Each player can take home
an 8x10 of one of our Best Dead Movie Stars.

Winter's last freeze is a nasty.
Lines are down, trains. Loop saloons can't manage the executives.
Sparkling trash races sleet down Wabash Avenue.
I beat the mob out; now I'm parked a few blocks south,
cozy in the suede of my brand-new '87 Cavalier.

Try it on, Sugarfoot? Warm your hands in mine
while mine stay warm in yours?
Later we can cut a song.
Never know what might go gold.

Positions of Strength

Chinese Proverb: *If you have to be a human being,
don't be a woman.*

On a street lined with sycamores and ginkgoes, as in Shanghai,
in a house with no pretext to strength, built high off the street
where dust hangs in the air like talcum in a ladies' dressing room,
there's a Siamese cat, a vase of hothouse flowers—birds of paradise—
and two women talking, as if not about themselves, about being women.

They talk about Indian women in their women's quarters
with their incense, silks, and English bric-a-brac.
There's no monsoon here, but it does rain.
The women are afraid of lingering colds; they speak of roofs, enclosures.
The subject of despair comes up; they hear disillusion
in the syllables of women's names; they see depth and darkness
in the slightest bit of wall or windowpane
or in any face, any landscape, anything.

If you have to be a human being, don't be a woman.
Your happiness and even your grief will depend on others
in whom you'll see things that may not be there.
Your self-possession will keep changing hands;
your endless battles—against dirt, friction, sobs like fists in your throat,
and spells of adoring sickness—will be yours alone.

Before any man had ever seen you, you wore short shorts,
drugstore cold cream squeezed from the ovaries of tortoises,
your mother's hot-pink lipstick, and mascara smudged with tears
because you didn't smell of calla lilies. You were stupid.

The cinnabar maple spread its branches at your upstairs window
when you moved your hands across a man.

Your foolishness increased.
You thought your wrists would snap, your inner walls collapse.
Yet it was his shoulder blades, fragile as a goat's, that you wept over.
No one ever cried like that for you; that's why you did it.

He'd pull a blanket over his nose,
and let nothing get to him, not even the dust—the hell with it.

You felt like a Tibetan girl of twenty
betrothed to a toddler Prince. You saw his limitations,
and found no way around them. You ended up with nothing
but a pregnancy you fixed and some postcards from Brazil.
Your self-disgust, you got back doubled.
When you woke up, it would hit you: "Rain again."
You'd lie there and imagine a catastrophe for him while he sat inside your rib cage
ridiculing you. His voice became your own: "You're weak!"

He had the nerve to think the house was waiting, not to mention
the cannisters and clocks, the linen and African flax.

Just because you stroked his feet, kissed his knees,
and carried him, a phantom baby, to full term.

The house tilts; dirt piles up against the back screen door.
Don't trust anyone. Most of all don't trust a woman with two faces, any woman
who, in all that nurturing, *needs* something.

Keep away from mothers huddling in the playground, interfering and indignant;

mothers who talk nonsense to their children and their husbands;

mothers who, when the kids finally stop crying, weep;

mothers who, when they've tricked the kids and husbands out of terrors,

will be left alone with their own fears.

    Tears in the carpet and curtains, tears in the soup and tea.

Never be a widow.

    Even if, like Indian women, you believe your husband

was the incarnation of a Hindu diety,

he won't leave you much: Walking pneumonia. The frostbound garden.

The house. A travel poster:

    Egypt, with her camels and feluccas;

with her banyans, their roots and branches fused;

and with lotus columns, pyramids, the Nile.

    Still it's cold out, close to the record.

The windows, iced with crystals, are no longer windows.

A couple of women talk to the fire, ask why it dies, ask why men

embrace them, erase them, use them to get born or get a leg up into heaven,

leaving them behind, Bodhisattvas at the gate,

and in the rain and cold of interiors that no man knows.

    There are no sexual mutilations here, no bride burnings.

Just two women talking.

Just one woman, really, with nothing left

but that she can still blush, fall in love, extend herself to anything

as if it were as sentient and complex as she.

    Nothing left but that when the columbine opens wide

and the trees seem female, she can cry for them.

For the delicate evergreens, and for the chestnut tree as it pulls itself to leaf again.

For any man, for each hour, for every brick and creature,
and for the dust that will be back every other day
on the street paved with oyster shells, in the faded yellow house
where a woman's glad to say
how much she had that she could give away.

Unsafe Havens

I was at home with someone—if I've ever been at home.
Now I bushwhack through a jungle.
Its canopy, though out of reach, doesn't seem that far from me.
It's an aerial garden
of berry cascades, leaf mosaics, petal fans,
and botarama branches hung with katydids,
bullet ants, bromeliads, and butterfly eggs:
lofty ceiling, little shelter

in a forest called Green Hell
that's hard to find or leave.
Rain bombards the espavels, collapses the mimosa bursts.
The moon moves through clouds, taking boundaries and landmarks.
Caught, lost, cut off by a limestone cliff
dripping venomous calyxes—I got across;
hand by hand, I climbed my trouser legs
up that wall.

I could measure anything. With sleeves, shoestrings, mango pits.
I stacked up well against whatever crossed my territory: ouakari, toucan, sloth,
the old Conquistadores, and the new, foreign prospectors
rushing in for gold: I've rushed with *them* from sudden rain
into their huts of branches, let their sweet water please my mouth,
then turned around and scorned them: "ambitious fishermen!"
They move in for their catch, and move on to the next,
poisoning, from far upstream, what river there is left.

Penetrating dense vegetation inch by inch, I've been confident, as if
I could see ahead of me.

But on the peaks, enclosing puffs of jungle: fortress walls,
crumbling in the rain.

Down below, stolen from the forest: forsaken squares of clover,
stripped by rain.

At the river's edge, where the giant pines domino:
rain. Always more.

Anthurium hearts and hand-shaped breadfruit leaves reach for me;
I still breathe the sweet, narcotic breath of all-night flowerfalls.

But now I'd give the whole, soaked, emerald-walled bazaar
of parrots, pigs, and monkeys
if the one I never meant to hurt,
whose voice I never heard,
could tell me why paradise can't be paradise
without regret, exhaustion, dread, and twenty feet a year of rain.

The cloud forest can't be unconfused.
Rain can't make her threats and gifts less repetitiously.
There's no haven safe from me.
Crouched with bullfrogs, fishing with banana bait
while yellow pippins dance around a cypress
twisted agonizingly as if it's giving birth,
I see two ways out of here: Retrace my steps.
Or stay—and watch the whole rainforest become a different place.

The jade tree's shakiness may look like courage there.
Forest surgeon, I could graft
patches of my arm skin onto failing cassia trees:
bit by bit, I'll be part of them and they of me.

One day, I'll make it all the way, in a hollow palm,
downriver to the ocean,
where the rain goes home to drown,
and where I'm done
with my jungle, its illuminations.

Spiraling Upward

Call it the worst ice storm since the storm of '48,
which was the worst since the storm of '24.
Overturned utility poles, evergreens in lace, a locked-up university.

I was stuck inside, in a lightless lecture hall with a sixty-ish professor
wearing little-tramp trousers and, up his sleeves, big themes.
Back and forth he paced, examining the ways the universe repeats itself:
the resemblances among microcosmic forms and patterns,
macrocosmic stellar ones, and hundreds in between.
DNA spiraled like a snailshell, a tornado, a galaxy, or the highest circle
of whirling powers—call it what I wanted to: The Abyss; Mystery; God.

I'm no intellectual, but I think a lot.
Love gets me started. I turn it around and around in my brain
as if it's meant to embrace everything.
Though walking around with my golden rule, I've met up with frauds
perpetrated by the winds, the government, my thoughts, and felt like a trespasser
everywhere I've been. I've gotten disenchanted with nature's great achievements:
even clouds too often played too rough.

How long would it take to rescue us? The professor
just kept working his parallells between the moods and weather, music and
   emotion.
He made me laugh.
As he spun abstractions out of facts as unassuming as a thumbprint,
I thought of Kepler's folly—that the planets' speeds made a diatonic scale.
And as he went on turning on his heels in front of me, left and right all night,
playing trombone with my brain, I began loving every syllable he spoke.

His fascination with sublimity made the dark enchanting.
Made that man a man with something I would call the "God" in man.
Kepler must have had it, as he labored toward the laws of planetary motion.
When the rescue truck showed up, I wasn't wondering how much longer.
It had taken days for me to master two plus two,
weeks to learn a tenor sax could turn me into dance.
Let it take all winter to conquer ice in time for spring.

In time for orange sunflowers to spiral from the earth,
as Voyager had done, while Voyager, given a gravitational boost from Jupiter,
ascends beyond the galaxy.
Snap! The lights are on.
I can't tell left from right, but out the unblocked door,
dodging fallen branches the professor—way ahead of me—had bounded over,
I'd begun thinking what I liked:

That he'd set a top spinning in my brain. That it won't stop.
That he gives big dimensions little pats, my Albert E.,
urging them to recognize what they have in common.
Time and space find each other
and the humble exaltations of that gorgeous intellect
are matched in my unelaborate feeling state.
Call it adoration.

Far from me, all those ageless, broadly gesturing teachers.
Though I've known them as long as I've known you
(in whom they live, whom you resemble, who resemble you).

You're always the same: removed from the world you've transfigured
with the phantom scales you play on your piano out in space.

I feel the notes: rain on snow.

As each near-perfect drop descends,
we send our thoughts shimmering toward
the credible heavens beyond, beyond the almost-hospitable sky.

Forever After

I lost faith in the truth when I was ten.
At twenty, I thought I had a clear idea of you.
What's happened—so fast!—is that we're no longer young.
We've marked our fifth visit to Four Corners,
our twenty-eighth June first.

It's "Middle Love": the unabashed devotion
that makes young love seem clumsy; the thanking heaven
every night at ten that it's not later; the moving fast
just to stay put.

• • •

Laramie, 8:00 A.M., June 1, 1996.
Our train pulls past the strata of churches, motels, stripjoints, fairs,
factories, farms, and villages.
Sitting next to me, you turn fifteen again.
You're chattering about a railroad in the East
built so fast by mules and men,
that one of them lies buried under every mile of track.

That had to be the Adirondack Line,
a fairy-tale railroad back in 1945:
passengers in chains of train cars starting in Malone
watched the ospreys, deer, and bear who waited by the tracks
to watch them go to Utica.

Now the line's long gone
to the few remaining kitfoxes and timberwolves.
Only an electric trolley, pulling one zebra-striped caboose,
bustles down the track anytime it has a mind to.

Meanwhile, we cross hot Nevada on this June midmorning.
I slow the too-fast scenery by staring into it, then let the train overtake
the desert. A couple of dust devils are outspinning the horizon.
Is nothing else happening?
You keep getting younger.

• • •

I want to sing my boy to sleep.
At eight, you'd rather be unaccompanied
as you fly past silos, barns, and irrigation ditches
of cornbelt spreads where lambs will soon be slaughtered.
A storm moves inland from the coast;
by the time it reaches Kansas, there's just rain enough
to drown the little turkeys opening their mouths to drink.
Your skinny chest
reminds me of the droughts of the depression.
Let water turn to needles in my throat, make it bleed,
but don't tell me a boy can vanish faster than a bird.

•••

4:00 P.M.: Our wavering train-beam slices the Blue Ridge.
Younger, younger, you'll soon sleep on a shelf.
Being a human baby, you're helpless.
You knit my belly, swell my breasts, cry when I say, "Soon."
See what's happened? Adoration.

All that happens after that, happens faster than before.
Counting to a hundred, I'm at ten;
I feel a spasm: you've moved into my womb.

Part of me forever after—
and you have it in you to be reborn of me.

•••

Sitting up in a sleeping car at 9 o'clock,
we speed past the asymmetrical valleys of North Georgia.
In the last sunrays of this first day of June, we see, against the clay
that makes the landscape rich and russet, small, meticulous groves.
Under every leaf of every miniature tree, gleams a tiny yellow peach.
    It's the loveliest spot so far. Still, I pray
that for our final destination, we'll be given
all the stops again. And that we'll be given back
tracks fast getting lost to orange hawkweed and blue chicory;
towns dying for a train;
fields where coyotes howl and huddle, though there's no storm yet,
only what will happen next, and that will happen faster
than any cyclone spinning for its life.

· · ·

Fast, then faster, we have crossed so many states together,
we can hardly think without thinking of each other
with a hopelessness inseparable from the magnanimous grace
that has brought us here, now, as the luxury
of our summer, our twenty-eighth, begins.

· · ·

I've been wrong, outrunning time.
I know how old we are, this June 1, 1996 at 8 o'clock A.M.
I can't lie about the truth.
In a shingle house just south of 54th Street in Chicago,
I have a husband tall as a door, chest like a tree, voice like a man's.
Give us this day, and I swear
there will be no end to the starting again.

While Morning's Part of Night

> *I am still completely a beginner at what I must become.*
> — Rilke

While morning's part of night, I start to spin out thoughts.
They flash like atoms in the blackness; soon, like molecules, they group.
Soon, cockatoos are crashing through a sunny jungle.
    Is that a flock of ibis on the coast? No, it's a city.
And far beyond the continent, some submarine volcanoes
give up their lives of violence to become the South Sea Islands.
    I get around,

trekking toward the world, circling back
to reimagine it. My right, emotive brain-half
wants action.
    This A.M., I'm all trust. Here's the deal I signed on for:
    Love enough, get loved enough.
    Never happens. Sulks set in, then other moods I can't get out of: soon
I'm thigh-deep; soon, hip-high.

    Noon. Over my left shoulder,
earthquakes take T'ang Shan. On the right, a wall of rain
falls on the Yellow River. China, you've gone under!
    I dive for the Pacific, freestyle to San Francisco.
    Here, the land-dance churns together feldspar, metasediments:
Hello, Sierra Nevadas! The gold the diggers claw back out ricochets like starbursts,
founding cowboy towns, flipping flapjacks for the Union Army.

Civil Wars wrench my superego. As if, without me, there's no greed.
Except for me, Gray and Blue might settle for a wrestling match.
Yes, I'm in the center—though I'll soon be put back in my place:
End of the Line. Where I await my turn to be blood and muscle
just like those in front of me, just like those behind.
A century past that North/South mess, I'll take my Celia for iced tea
at Lester's restaurant. As if he'd pour ketchup over our two lovely colors!

Have I imagined something? No, I've looked Hate right in the knees.
Soon, my left, rational brain-half has perceived a pattern:
Over There, officers tortured human skin-sacks.
And when Professor E., writings burned and bounties on his head,
sailed our way, we dumped a double hate-load on Japan. Was *this*
a product of my mind, a bully at its kindest, twisting insights, cranking out
unthinkable realities? Now I've got hate to call my own—or maybe it's got me.

Back ahead to Georgia, '67: my sister drives; I ride; that's all that's been
decided as we sputter through Savannah's squares, pastels, iron lace, and wicker
in her new Tin Lizzie, toward a run-in with some bad old boys. I'd be spam in the can
for them, but Cynthia can cool-talk: we're soon two old girls again.
The good guy comes; I'm gone. I'm *The Dialogues'* "beloved": The one of two
who loves the more, and then is loved the more. And then loves more,
then more, is replenished in proportion to what's been given over

to a force too substantial to be touched.
Still, any instance of this love is just a metaphor for Love,
which, with one hand, tilts the earth
and with the other, twirls it.
Soon I'm hurtling toward the Midwest. Back in Georgia, Mamma's baby firs
unfurl, bright chartreuse against the balsams' bottle green.
Soon after that, in New York City, Cynthia has Dan, then Sam.

Break's over! War's back on. My P.M. was two shakes long.

Bosnia, I'm for you. It's our sea, Refugees.

Catastrophe, those your toes I'm not supposed

to notice just offstage?

Daddy's homemade radio brings tones of saxophones,

falling toward the falling notes

of longed-for rain,

late in the day.

It's early.

Cynthia has Joe and Emma.

I'm new, too. I'm thinking

with both my hemispheres.

Chicago, you've got me surrounded

with expectant faces. And right here in front of us,

a large chunk of time

is beginning to crack open—

Chopsticks on a Vase

Each leaf falls as if it were motioning, "No."
. . . This hand here is falling.
And look at the other one. . . . It's in them all. . . .
— Rilke, "Autumn"

From a distance, the platform seems to swing into the distance.
I came here by train; I'll take one last train away.

He's with me, as if we might be setting off again
for the *ville fortifiée* where we could live,
if we could live in it.

I'm here, just as I've been
when I've thrown my life away, and when I snatched it back.
    That's how I spent it?
    Not quite yet—and in immense happiness,
kissing pages from *Swann's Way* to *The Past Recaptured*.
    In our stronghold/haven,
we gave each other centuries to live—
if we could live on histories and myths.

In a Ming Romance, a Bodhisattva plucks, with gold chopsticks,
one crystal chip from a celestial crystal vase: That's a snowfall.

That explains the white, sixteenth-inch ballerinas
making shimmering entrances into here, now:
mid-west, mid-December, mid-sunset—

Or is it drizzling chickdown, or sprinkling willow floss?
Or snowing cotton gossamers, or raining lithium salt?

"Stop the thought-flights!" I call out, and retort, "Stop 'Stopping' them!
"What happened when astronomers cleared the heavens of circles?"
"A fresh ellipsis wobbled in and looped new loops around the spheres."
"What embraces windhovers, stockbrokers, spaceships, and Australia?"
"Nothing less than anyone's unstopped imagination."
"Let's keep this backtalk up as long as possible."

On the no-snow days, the Bodhisattva taps a dancebeat on the vase
to keep the planet just off-balance, on her toes, revolving.

By "Whole World," I mean the person with me here, now.
He knows what's behind the magnetic storms that mastermind
the blackouts of our radios: nothing less than the Pole's spectacular aurorae.
Who controls the blackness that wraps whole hemispheres?
It swirls on every surface, and in and out of ballroom gowns, laboratories,
motorboats, Spanish moss, and turnpike cloverleaves. Suddenly, it's bottlenecked
at my stage door, about to rush me, smother, crush me,
make me breathe it, drink it up.

Oh, to break my *rendez-vous* with that dark animal—
To hold, for two days more, the lit-up life I've spent my life
imagining to life—

In a dream last night, I found my Love
in the blue-green suitcase that we took with us to Africa and Fiji.
Within that dream, I dreamed he lost the suitcase—me.
I woke up praying, "Train, don't make me miss him—
he's my train for glory."

One day, one tap: *the vase shatters; earth sinks*
in powdered sugar, talcum powder, pear pollen, powder sand . . .

My reservation's fixed: *Lower (No Dreams) Berth.*

En rose, in the distance, the sun slips behind the tracks,
which merge to go the distance. I've got no strength, but I can see
the air, crystal-bright and thick with white, begin to waver.
    Look what's here: It's nothing more
than a comet-studded colt, about to bolt for There.

My husband says, "Be me and stay."

After that, no sound. No cold. No ice-taste on my lips,
which brush no cloud of breath and powder snow. If I could talk,
I'd call myself "Sweetheart." I'd say,

"*Whole World, Sweetheart, I've got no sky, no ground, no blur—*
just one shaft of sunlight from one morning, one July:
    It held us, as we fell together, as we held each other.
    Salt on your lips, you kissed me in the low, quiet tide,
while time sifted, bit by bit,
through the hole at the end of the ocean."